Expressions of Soul

Clayton

BALBOA
PRESS
A DIVISION OF HAY HOUSE

Copyright © 2010 Clayton

All rights reserved. No part of this book may be used or reproduced by any means, graphic, electronic, or mechanical, including photocopying, recording, taping or by any information storage retrieval system without the written permission of the publisher except in the case of brief quotations embodied in critical articles and reviews.

Balboa Press books may be ordered through booksellers or by contacting:

Balboa Press
A Division of Hay House
1663 Liberty Drive
Bloomington, IN 47403
www.balboapress.com
1-(877) 407-4847

Because of the dynamic nature of the Internet, any Web addresses or links contained in this book may have changed since publication and may no longer be valid. The views expressed in this work are solely those of the author and do not necessarily reflect the views of the publisher, and the publisher hereby disclaims any responsibility for them.

The author of this book does not dispense medical advice or prescribe the use of any technique as a form of treatment for physical, emotional, or medical problems without the advice of a physician, either directly or indirectly. The intent of the author is only to offer information of a general nature to help you in your quest for emotional and spiritual well-being. In the event you use any of the information in this book for yourself, which is your constitutional right, the author and the publisher assume no responsibility for your actions.

Any people depicted in stock imagery provided by Thinkstock are models, and such images are being used for illustrative purposes only.
Certain stock imagery © Thinkstock.

ISBN: 978-1-4525-0113-0 (sc)
ISBN: 978-1-45250-115-4 (hc)
ISBN: 978-1-4525-0114-7 (e)

Library of Congress Control Number: 2010916721

Printed in the United States of America

Balboa Press rev. date: 11/12/2010

This book is dedicated to those who led the
way and to those upon the search.

Introduction

My writing is raw and from my guts and my heart. It began in 1998, and now seems the time to share it. These words reflect the changes that occurred as I began to evolve into a spiritual being and experience the awakening of the divine within myself. I have always felt the words within this book, but I refused to acknowledge them for thirty-five years of my life. The most important thing I have learned in the past twelve years is that when change is coming, embrace it with life, love, and positive thoughts. Do your best to go with the flow and follow your inner guidance. Do the best you can to stay linked to divine inspiration and to tap into the guidance that comes from a higher source.

Everything you read in these pages came from a higher and inner source .The words came to me through dreams and in times of silent meditation while l was going through some very difficult life changes. I used to sing a little phrase from an old Bobby Bare tune that went like this: "Drop-kick me, Jesus, through the goalpost of life." In other words, be careful what you ask for, because you will get it.

As you read these words, open your mind, your body, and your spirit to receive whatever messages are waiting for you … and enjoy the journey.

Acknowledgments

I'd like to thank the following people for their support and love:

Cindy Gardner, my spiritual teacher, who has helped me in my spiritual growth and my spiritual awakening. She helped me as I climbed the mountains only to topple off the peaks and helped me as I crawled through the valleys to climb the mountains again. If ever an angel walked this earth, it is Cindy.

My daughter Amanda who was there in every way for her dad and who gave time and effort to help me see this book through to the finish.

My daughter Christine whose love and support has meant so much to me through the years.

Teresa Nicodemus at Balboa Press, whose statement "stiletto heels and a cowboy hat" let me know that I'd made the right connection.

And finally, all the people who have passed through my life to play their parts in my awakening.

In love and light,

Clayton

Contents

Introduction vii
Acknowledgments ix

Soul Scenes 1
   Do You Hear? 2
   The Rose 3
   My Dreams 4
   My Shadowed Mind 5
   Dreams 6
   Night Scenes 7
   Voices 8
   Twist of Time 9
   My Mind 10
   Another Time 11
   Just a Glimpse 12

Within 13
   Higher Consciousness 14
   Inner Peace 15
   Who I Am 16
   Awareness 17
   Hope 18
   Clarity 19
   Lightness 20
   Shackles 21
   Caged Dove 22
   Life's Highway 23
   Trail of Memories 24

A Deeper Look 25
   Morning Cries 26
   Look Within 27
   A Lifeless Thing 28
   Grassy Plains 29
   The Battle 30
   In My Eyes 31

 Silence 32
 Prayer of Forgiveness 33
Heartfelt. 35
 The Act of Love 36
 Acceptance. 37
 Power of Love 38
 Emotion 39
 The Brightened Path 40
 Unconditional Love 41
 Presence. 42
 Meaning to My Life 43
 Vision 44
 As I Watch You Sleep 45
 Awaken 46
 First Touch. 47
 Mistaken 48
 A Love Like Mine 49
 Spending Time 51
 Severed 52
 I Know I Said 53
 Golden Bands 54
 Communion 55
 The Key. 56
 The World Would Understand. 57
 My Special Friend 58
 Silent Stare. 60
 The Choice 61
 Three Wishes 62
 Alone in Love 63
 Your Picture. 64
 Imprisoned 65
 Lost Moments 66
 Trust 67
 Changes of Your Heart. 68
 Reunion. 69
 Nameless 70
 You and I. 71

Crossing Over 73
    Death 74
    Don't Cry 75
    Last Ride 76
Angels and Spirit Guides 77
    Whispers 78
    Lonely Post 79
    The Chamber... 80
    Angels 81
    My Thoughts of You 82
Words to Inspire... 83
    Lifetime.. 84
    Love of Life 85
    Secrets 86
    Time 87
    Perfection 88
    Release.. 89
    Believe.. 90
    Limits 91
    I Am 92
    Cosmic Winds... 93
    The Man Behind the Wood 94
Paths That Crossed.. 95
    Expression of You 96
    Unveiling.. 97
    Thoughts of You 98
    Reality of the Heart 99
    Never in My Life 101
    Two Hearts 102
    If I Could 103
    You Already Have Me 104
    Awaiting the Call (A Prince in a Fairy Tale)................ 105

Soul Scenes

Do You Hear?

Do you hear me when I call upon you,
or do my prayers fall on deafened ears?

Do you hear me when I go in silent meditation
in search of release from my confusion and my fears?

Do you hear me when I call upon you
in search of answers to the questions that I have asked?

Do you hear me while I sit in silent meditation,
and I call upon the ancient gods, the gods they say are now long past?

Do you see me when my head is held in my hands
while tears stream down my face?

Do you see me when my heart is heavy from the sadness and the pain,
even though in meditation I begin to feel there is no gain?

Do you hear me while I participate in the practice of my faith,
or are my prayers and meditation floating out in empty space?

I call upon the ancient gods, the gods who have gone before,
to listen to this humble man while his faith is once again restored.

Do you hear me? Do you see me while I sit in silent prayer,
or do my meditations fall on deafened ears?
Do you see and feel my anguish and my pain
while I feel in this lifetime there is nothing left to gain?

I seek the answers to my questions from a higher, truer source.
All I ask of spirit is to assist me on this course.

Do you hear me? Do you see me while the tears stream down my face,
or do my prayers go unanswered while floating out in empty space?

The Rose

While traveling through the barren landscapes of my dreams,
I came upon a single perfect rose.
It seemed such an odd place for such a perfect flower.
There seemed to be nothing but sand and
sun, in a place that had no end.
I felt no breeze, I heard no sound, no movement did I sense.
I slowly settled down and sat beside this single rose.
I cast my gaze upon it, watching with intent.
I had the strangest feeling this rose was heaven-sent.
I began to notice little things about this single rose;
the stem was strong and straight, the leaves, each one perfect in its shape,
andthere was brilliance in the color of every petal
and how perfectly each was placed.
It still strikes me as a strange and lonely place for my rose and I to be,
but maybe one day, through enlightenment, the
answer to this mystery will be revealed to me.

My Dreams

The kiss we shared last night in my silent dreams
still lingers on my lips. A reality it seems.
The gentle touch of your sweet love, that you share with me in dreams,
still tingles on my fingertips, carried over from my dreams.
I still can feel the pressure from the gentle swelling of your breast
as I held and pressed you gently toward the hunger in my chest.
The gentle movements that we shared as, in tender love, we joined,
seemed so real, the dream has somehow come
into the consciousness of my mind.
These treasured dreams I have of you, that fill my lonely night,
I know one day will become my wakeful reality.

My Shadowed Mind

I look beyond the shadows and see the figures in the night.
They gather all around me with silent, empty stares.
At times they bring me happiness. At times they terrorize my nights.

I look beyond the shadows and see the fleeting figures in the night.
I pray that dawn will quickly come to help ease my tortured mind.
The darkness passes oh, so slowly, the whispers I still hear.
They are the voices of the past, memories now long dead.
They still quietly creep into the chambers that dwell inside my head.

I pray that dawn will quickly come and bring with it the light
that will once again release me from my fears and demons in the night.

Dreams

Dreams are the subconscious desires that lay
within the heart of a woman or a man.
The man has dreams of one day gazing into the eyes of the woman.
The man has dreams of one day gently holding and caressing the woman
who holds his heart and soul.
The man dreams of the woman he loves.
The dreams of the woman are as yet unknown to the man.
The vision of you fills my dreams.

Night Scenes

I hear the voices in the night, these things that we call dreams.
Listen close, pay attention to these nightly inner scenes,
for if you do you're sure to find a message from your higher being.

Voices

As I stand with trembling hand upon this ancient latch,
I hear the voices from within, calling, calling, "Come look, come see."
The voices come in whispers, never do they shout.
You will hear their silent murmurs if you listen with intent.
They are only here to help you cast away your fears and angers
and release your inner doubts.
Slowly, I push open the door. There's just silence from within.
"Come look, come see, there is nothing here to fear,
for I am you and you are me. Come in, come look, come see."

Twist of Time

He was sitting on a bridge, just below a castle wall,
in shadow, yet in light. The scene I still recall.
I knew him in an instant as well as he knew me,
for through some twist of time, for just a brief moment,
I was allowed to see another time, another place long past.
I was shown, for just a moment, another man, another form
of the man I used to be.

My Mind

What's going on inside my mind, a mind
that doesn't seem to be my own?
It seems to want to travel to memories and
places I wouldn't call my own.
But everywhere it travels I have a sense of going home.
It seems to come and go with a will that's not my own.
I only pray each time it leaves, it remembers to come home.

Another Time

Do I know you?
Have we met somewhere before?
Even though I've never seen you in this time,
I feel we've met somewhere before.
If I let you look into my eyes, and you let me look into yours,
maybe we can find the times and lives that we have shared before.
I know our present forms are different than
the forms of other times we wore,
so let's just look into each other's eyes to find
the times and lives we shared before.
I know I feel this kinship of another place and time,
for both our souls just stop and stare as we both seem to share
a memory from another time, now long past.
Wait! Don't go! Don't stop this soulful gaze.
Alas, you've turned, you've left,
and now the memories of a long-lost past return to a foggy haze.

Just a Glimpse

Just a glimpse is all we were given, a chance to
see what once was and can be again.
A moment when the portals of time opened to
allow us to see a love that once was
and is again.

A love so strong that it has transcended time to
live once more on this earthly plain.
A love so strong and magnetic that after both lives had passed,
it lived on to be reborn anew.

How wonderfully magnificent is a universe
that allows us to see what once was
and is again.

My dearest one, how can we ever feel anything
but love and devotion for each other
if there are forces like this that brought us back together?

In a twinkling of an eye, we were shown two people
in different lives and different times;
one so willing to love, the other so afraid to try.

Alas, here we are again in a different time and, yes, in different lives
yet in circumstances so much the same; one so
willing to love, the other so afraid to try.

My dearest love, allow us this life to share our love and our hearts
throughout all eternity.

Within

Higher Consciousness

We've all been here before, and some of us will
return for more lessons yet unlearned
for reasons we refuse to see or try to comprehend.
Perhaps it's fear of knowing more than we feel we are able to believe,
but if you allow your mind to wander and allow your thoughts to expand
through sudden insights and awareness we will come to understand
that by attaining a higher consciousness,
we can improve the situations for all of mortal man.

Inner Peace

As I saddle up old Sundance, there's a trail I hope to find.
The trail to inner freedom, the trail to peace of mind.
As I saddle up old Sundance and pull the cinch up tight,
I know the trail I'm looking for will bring
me peace and sleep-filled nights.
The trail I will be taking is not one you can really see,
for the trail I will be taking starts and ends inside of me.
The trail I will travel will take me deep inside the man.
I start this sacred quest to find the man I truly am.
The trail I travel over is a vision in my mind.
It takes me through the valleys and mountains
to the inner peace I hope to find.
I know there is a path to healing the spirit and the mind
as I ride along on Sundance and this trail I long to find.
I go in search of understanding, in search of my sacred self,
and once I find this trail to the inner peace I seek,
I'll travel back and try to guide others on their
trails, to find happiness and true relief.

Who I Am

I am a soul in search of love, integrity, and truth.
I am a soul in search of knowledge, wisdom,
and a way to serve others in this life.
I am a soul in search of meaning, a soul just
speaking out in hope of being understood.
I am a soul in search of enlightenment, serenity, and purpose to my life.
I am a soul in search of patience, faith and trust, tolerance and peace.
I am a soul in search of guidance, in trying to find the way
to make this journey a little easier for those
behind me than those who led the way.

Awareness

Awareness is a blessed gift that comes from within yourself.
So when you're filled with questions, with answers you can't find,
go off into the power, the power of your mind.
You will find the answers there; they lie within yourself.
So go and find some solitude, a place to be alone.
Now sit in peaceful quiet, stop the chatter of the conscious self.
It's time to go even deeper inside your sacred self
and dust off all the knowledge that's been stacked there on the shelf.
To your questions you'll find the answers,
so take this inner journey and seek your higher self.

Hope

I sit upon my saddle and watch the cattle graze.
I hear their gentle movements, and my tensions start to fade.
As I sit and watch them moving, from here to there, never in a rush,
I let my mind go wandering to places far away.
I find myself drifting across these grassy slopes
to days when I was younger, my heart still filled with hope.

I watch the days start turning back to times that have long since passed.
I see the child I used to be; it makes me hunger for the past.
I know I can't go back there. The past holds no place for me.
The future is where I'm heading. There's
really nothing in the past for me.

The past is only simple memories of things that used to be.
The future's where I'm heading. Want to ride along with me?

Clarity

Clear the fog, push through the haze, find your clarity.
Open up and look inside, traverse your troubled mind.
Release your fears, release your past, for once you do
you will find the riches of your mind have been waiting there for you.

Lightness

There's a lightness in my heart that I have not felt in years.
It finally came to be by releasing my obsessions and my fears.
The joy of life has finally come through the cleansing power of my tears.
It seems at times it took forever, a multitude of years.

The light of love that now shines for all the world to see
is the beacon that is saying, you need not have any fear of me,
for the power of my love shines forth for everyone to see.

So I hope you all have patience and try to understand
that I no longer have the desire to make my living off the land.
So I hope you all have patience and try to understand
that I am going on a journey to help my fellow man

Shackles

Do you fear to face your future? Are you
fearful of events you can't yet see?
Do you cling to a past that was lonely, full of heartache and pain?
Throw off those binding shackles and step up to a higher plane.
Boldly grasp your future and all that's there for you to gain.

Caged Dove

I held within my hand for years a gentle, fragile dove
who shared with me her purity and showered me with love.
But through my insecurities, jealousies, and
fears, I slowly clipped her wings.
It was not my intention to cage this gentle dove,
but still I built her prison through my lack of
understanding of how to freely love.
Yet through some source of power that was much greater than my own,
I left the cage door open, and my dove flew away from home.
I pray that one day she'll come back as she starts to understand
that her leaving sent me on a journey of my own.
The journey that I started on took me inside this fearful, angry man.
It brought to me knowledge as I came to understand
that before I could freely love another,
first I would have to freely learn to love the inner man.

Life's Highway

While I travel down life's highway, I go searching through my mind.
I'm trying to find a better place, a better space in time.
Old memories try to haunt me with visions from the past.
I know they're just memories, and old memories never last.

As I travel down life's highway, I'm searching for my place,
the place that will bring new purpose and meaning to my life.
I'm searching for the reasons, the reasons why I'm here.
I'm standing at the crossroads, but which path am I to take?

While I travel down life's highway, the
memories I thought I'd left behind
are always in pursuit of me, no rest they'll let me find.
I'm standing at the crossroads, trying to make the proper choice,
the road that will give me liberation and freedom from the past.

Trail of Memories

I ride the trail of memories with an aching in my chest,
a heart that seems so heavy and thoughts that never give me rest.

I ride the trail of memories as tears run down my face.
I'm looking for some place to hide, somewhere to heal my wounds.

I ride the trail of memories with pain I cannot hide,
with a longing that never leaves me, sorrow always at my side.

I ride the trail of memories and cuss my cursed truths,
for the things I should have said and done but
hadn't learned yet in my youth.

I ride the trail of memories, trying to heal my grief,
this place I fear I will never find, somewhere to find relief.

So I will ride the trail of memories until I find my inner peace.

A Deeper Look

Morning Cries

While I listen to the morning cries of the turtle dove,
I sit and let my thoughts reflect on where our love went wrong.
Their morning songs begin to cause a stirring deep inside my soul
as I begin to search for answers I know are hidden there.
And as my tears begin to fall, I come to realize
the reasons for the love I lost
were through my inabilities to face my fears
and demons at such a terrible cost.
The demons that have twisted and torn at the very essence of my being
became such a part of me, they were like a living thing.
I started to believe all hope was gone, that for me there was nothing left.
But through some inner power, of which I did not know was there,
I rose above my sorrows to drink in fresh, cool air.
So if you start to feel all hope is gone, look inside
yourself and you will come to see
that the power of real love lies inside. Go take a look and see.
So I will share my thoughts on this with you:
to truly love another, the love begins with you.

Look Within

We're all looking for the answers, just trying to find some clues,
to help us get through this life without being
beaten, mistreated, or abused.
You will not find the answers in the outer world of man.
You have to turn around and look inside the inner self to understand.
We're all just looking for someone we can love
and to share our hopes and dreams.

A Lifeless Thing

There stands a lonely, battered, and beaten wind-swept tree
where once there stood a mighty oak.
Now all that's left is a shell that's been stripped of its armor and its cloak.
A weathered, beaten remnant of what once was the master of the hill.
The majesty and splendor no longer can you see.
It's just a broken, withered, lifeless thing
that cries out from inside of me.

Grassy Plains

We stood upon a battlefield, with swords clutched tightly in our hands.
I can still recall the way the sunlight danced across your battle dress.
I still recall marking the vital spot where my
sword would pierce your chest.
Then came the call for battle!

How boldly we both charged across the grassy plain.
I remember in an instant, the terrible stabbing pain,
for your sword had found the spot you had
marked from across the grassy plain.
I can still recall the terror and relief upon your face.
The terror for the life you took, the relief that you still lived.

The Battle

I have battled with confusion, bitterness, and strife,
a continuous war I have been waging against my inner life.
My ego has been the victor throughout the first four decades of my life,
until I came to find out, ego was the cause of all the bitterness and strife.
The ego wants to keep us frightened, wary, and confused.
It does not want us to come to understand
that the outer shell we look upon is not the true essence of man.
The ego never gives us peace.
It seems to thrive upon the turmoil of self-hatred and self-doubt.
The ego fights the battle to keep us in control,
for it does not want us to look within to find the truthfulness of soul.
The ego knows once you start the journey to find your inner self,
to seek a higher knowledge, to seek your higher self,
for once you do, it won't be long before ego is cast upon the shelf.

In My Eyes

Do not look upon this shell, this shell of mortal man.
You need to look into my eyes, to the soul of who I am.
So I ask you not to judge the physical me
but to take a closer look at the man inside of me.
Although my outward appearance may not be pleasing to your senses,
all I ask is that you take one brief look into my gentle eyes
to see the soul of who I am.

Silence

In silence you will find your inner peace and relaxation from the race.
In silence you will come to learn that the changes in your life
happen at a necessary pace.

In silence you will come to see that in your peaceful quiet times,
you can find the path that leads to peace, contentment, and harmony.

In the silent peaceful times, you may feel abandoned and alone,
but through faith and understanding, you'll find your way back home.

So take some quiet moments and analyze your fears,
then just wash them all away with the cleansing flow of tears.

Give yourself a warm embrace, a gentle tender hug,
for we are never truly all alone.

Prayer of Forgiveness

I've given you great sorrow. I know I've caused you pain.
And I know you won't believe this, but I've caused myself the same.
The pain is every bit as real for me as it is for you.
I've tried everything to bring you home, but
I know your heart is hurting still.
So I will give you space and give you time to heal.
I only have one thing to ask of you, my love;
that is not to look upon the outer man
but to look into my eyes to see the man that I now am.
The man that caused us sorrow, the man that caused us pain,
no longer walks among us, for he's no longer here.
The man you see before you now, you will never have to fear.
For his love for you is simple, but it is pure and it is true,
and if you don't believe this, I ask this now of you,
to look into these eyes to see the man I am.
So, my love, just look into these eyes to see the man I am.

Heartfelt

The Act of Love

The act of love is the willingness to give more than you take.
To return more than you receive.
To share your thoughts and feelings freely, without fear.
To console and to aid in your friends' time of need.
To offer strength and understanding in times
of their confusion and their fear.
To stand firmly beside each other in times of trial and despair.
And to always keep in mind that you are equal partners in this life.

Acceptance

When you fall in love with someone, remember that it is the person
you see before you now that you love,
not the mirror image of someone you think that they should be.
When you fall in love with me, take me as I am.
Do not try to change me into other than I am.

Power of Love

The power of love is a gift from above
that is to be cherished and nurtured for it to grow.
The power of love is the radiance of compassion and understanding
that is openly shared by two hearts.
The power of love is a gift that is given to us all.
The power of love gives us an inner light that helps
to brighten our days and our nights
as we walk hand in hand through our daily lives.

Emotion

The emotion of love can be fleeting or everlasting.
The emotion of love that flees quickly is not true.
The emotion of love that stays through the
good times and the bad is eternal.
The emotion of true love may bend, but it will never break.
The emotion of true love is allowing each other
the freedom to grow and expand,
without fear of reprisal.
It is the understanding that we are both individuals,
both knowing that we have our own spiritual paths to take.
So have faith in your love for each other and know within your hearts
that even in times of separation the bonds of love, trust, and faith
will always bring you home.

The Brightened Path

The way the moon rises over the treetops in the evening sky
to brighten the paths we travel by night
is the way the light of my love shines to brighten your path.
As you travel through times of confusion and fear,
the light of my love is always with you,
to brighten the darkness you feel surrounds you.
The light of my love will never leave you unprotected or alone,
for I am always with you.

Unconditional Love

If love is unconditional, then that's what I feel right now.
If life is just a passing glimpse, then let me share that glimpse with you.
If love is what I feel inside, then let me share
that love with you for eternity.
Love can be expressed through many emotions—
fear, jealousy, frustration, and mistrust—
if not truly understood.

But the true expressions of love are the freedom
to give to each other, share ideas,
to talk openly with each other, without fear of being hurt.
Love is the joy in being one with each other, whether near or apart.
It's the feeling that each kiss or touch is just as wonderful as the first,
that every moment spent together should be
treated like it could be the last.

Through my fear and frustrations, I have wandered
like a man lost, confused, and dazed.
Like a lonely soul, I've been fighting through a thick and heavy haze.

Love is such a range of emotions, it's hard to name them all,
but this much I can assure you, each one of them I've felt.

Presence

If there is a heaven, then it is when I am in your presence.
If there is a hell, then it is when we are apart.
The time we spend together means so much,
just to share a simple smile or the tenderness of your touch.
To me you are the sunset and the rising moon.
You are feminine grace and beauty, with an
inner strength beyond compare.
You are an angel sent form God above,
who has so graciously shared with me her love.
To me you are the stars that twinkle in the skies above,
and every time I look at you my heart could
burst from the passion and the love.
You are my tender angel sent from God above.

Meaning to My Life

The day you said you'd marry me and said you'd be my wife,
you filled my heart with gladness and you brought meaning to my life.
I know we've been through hardships, trials, and despair.
I am sorry for the sadness, the confusion, and the pain.
Your love, trust, and friendship is what I hope to reattain.
For even though we're parted now and no longer side by side,
in the quiet places in my heart you will always be my bride.

The day you said you'd marry me and said you'd be my wife,
you filled my heart with gladness and you brought meaning to my life.
And though the distance that divides us sometimes seems so great,
I now surrender all I am to love, destiny, and fate.
I place my love before you. That is all I have to give,
so I pray you take this offer and allow my heart to live.

The day you said you'd marry me and said you'd be my wife,
you filled my heart with gladness and you brought meaning to my life.
The day you said you'd marry me, I promised you my life.

Vision

You are my vision splendor, my angel draped in white.
I gaze upon your picture each and every night.

You are my vision splendor, my angel draped in white.
I kiss and hold you in my dreams, all through my lonely nights.

You are my vision splendor, the woman I adore.
The only gift I have to offer you is pure love forever more.

You are my vision splendor, my angel draped in white.
We will dance again together in my dreams of you tonight.

As I Watch You Sleep

As I lay beside you and watch you in your sleep,
my soul is flooded by the love and joy you have brought into my life.

As I lay beside you and watch you in your sleep,
I have a strong desire to make things better
and more pleasurable for you.

As I lay beside you and watch you in your sleep,
I gently caress your cheek, and I have a deep
desire to love and give you more.

As I lay beside you and watch you in your sleep,
I gaze with wonder at your beauty and your strength.

As I lay beside you and watch you in your sleep,
I am reminded of how much of yourself you have given all to me.

As I lay beside you and watch you in your sleep,
I move to hold you closer just to feel your warmth and tenderness.

As I lay beside you and watch you in your sleep,
I gently embrace each tender moment of the life that we have shared.

As I lay beside you and watch you in your sleep,
I gently pull you to my chest when I feel you snuggle close.
Then the tears of my desire for you flow with love.

As I lay beside you and watch you in your sleep,
I gently kiss your face. I am yours forever.

Awaken

As I awaken from my slumber, my first thoughts are of you.
As I look upon the woman of my dreams and my desires,
I am touched by the graceful beauty in your face
and the sensuous lines and curves that form your shape.
My mind becomes intoxicated by your tender scent.
I am stirred by rising passion, but still I wait,
for I do not wish to interrupt the dreams that are playing in your sleep.

First Touch

From the first time I placed trembling, searching
fingers upon your tender thigh,
you captured my heart like a long-held breath,
that became a long and loving sigh.
I shall never forget the taste of our first kiss
or the sweet and tender feeling of you skin.
As we released the hunger we both held within,
the passion that we'd been denied
came bursting forth like thunder as the
lightening played across our minds.
We held and clung to each other, our passion running high.
With every kiss and gentle touch, a love burst
forth that no longer would be denied.
Like a fire burning out of control, nothing will ever put out the flames.
Our passion and desire no longer could we hide,
for every chance and moment, together did we lay in love's embrace.
I placed gentle kisses on your soft and tender flesh.
Your sweet and secret places I did taste.
We held each other for hours, for neither one
wanted our time to ever come to an end.
The days turned into weeks, the weeks turned into months,
and now the years have passed,
but my love and desire for you, for all eternity, shall ever last.

Mistaken

Could I have been mistaken, or maybe just confused,
when I read the words "I love you" in your little note?
Could I have been mistaken, or just a bit confused,
when you signed that you were mine?
Oh, how my heart began to pound from the power of those words.
My tears fell down like raindrops from a rejoicing and delighted soul.
Please, do not be afraid, my love, to trust my longing heart,
for I will stand beside you. Never will I depart.
All I have to offer is my gentle, loving heart.
I promise I will always treat your love so
tenderly, I will handle it with care,
for there's no one else on this good earth that could ever be compared
to the woman that you are or the love we have to share.

A Love Like Mine

You may seek and you may search, but a love
like mine you will never find.
You can run and try to hide, but a love this true cannot be denied.

I feel we have waited lifetimes as we venture through this life.
We each have our fears and our issues of mistrust.
But this much I will promise you,
I will love you until all that's left of me is dust.

My precious, gentle angel that God has sent my way,
I know that if we try, our love will never fade away.

As I sit here in this moment, I ask the angels for the proper words to say,
for I fear that if they're the wrong ones, you will only run away.

With every passing moment you are at the forefront of my thoughts.
With every passing moment my love for you grows stronger,
even though we no longer ever touch.

I hold so tightly in my heart a picture of your face,
a face that's blessed by beauty, tenderness, and grace.

I will always treat your love like a tender, fragile dove,
for I know that you were sent to me from the heavens up above.

I sit in silent meditation as I write these words to you,
with a prayer that in some way the feelings I have for you
will come shining through.

As I sit and write these words they seem so
inadequate of what I really feel,
when all I really want to say is my love for you is real.

How can I express to you the way my love burns like a fire in my chest?
You are always in my thoughts, my love, and I pray that you are happy
and that I have not in some way caused your unhappiness or unrest.

I love you, little one, and will always proudly stand
beside you like no others in my life,
for as you already know, before I ever let harm
come to you I'd gladly give my life.

So let's please break these chains that bind us
from having our everlasting love,
for your heart and love, like a gentle flower, I will hold so tenderly
within the beatings of my heart.

I love you beyond all reason.

Spending Time

You never have to thank me for spending time with you,
for there's nothing else on this green earth that I would rather do.
Your love and your friendship are all that my heart craves,
for I know I will take these passions and desires with me to the grave.
Every moment you allow me to look upon your beauty and your grace
is all that I could ask for--- no one else could ever take your place.
My love for you is simple, but it is pure and it is true,
for there is nothing more I could ask from life
than just spending time with you.

Severed

Love cannot flourish if it is not nourished. Love
cannot survive if it is not shared.
If the roots of love are severed, then the blossoms of love begin to wither.
If the clouds of fear and cynicism block the life-
giving rays of the sunlight of love,
then the heart of the flower of love will surely die.

I Know I Said

I know I said I would never ask for more than you could give,
but all I am asking now is that you allow my heart to live.
Whenever we're together I work so hard to hold and to suppress
the ever-present passions and desires that rage
like fire inside my pounding chest.
Every time I look into those big blue eyes my
thoughts start spinning around,
and just the thought of your sweet kiss sends
me swirling round and round.
I love you more than words can say. How I wish I could
express the longing I have for you that never lets me rest.
I know as you read these words, once again you'll pull away,
but believe me when I say I understand your fear,
for it was me that brought it on you.
Please let it be me who takes your fear away.
My only wish is to once again feel the passion in your kiss,
to slowly run my hands along your shapely hips,
to nuzzle softly at your neck, and to kiss your tender lips.
Please don't be mad, my love. It is just the passion of your man,
but until you feel safe with me, I'll be happy just to hold your tiny hand.

Golden Bands

The golden bands we place upon our fingers are a symbol to the world
of our desire to share our thoughts, ideas,
fears, and triumphs with another.
The golden bands we place upon our fingers are a symbol to the world
of our desire to join as two, not to become one.
To remember that we are individuals, with
the desire to give the gift of love
equally to one another.
I pledge my gift of love to you on this most special of days.

Communion

Love is the communion between two souls,
always seeking the harmony and balance in their ideas and emotions.
They work together willingly, on equal and understanding terms,
where neither soul is above or below the other,
where both can walk hand in hand and shoulder to shoulder
throughout their daily and eternal journeys.

The Key

In your little, tiny hands you hold the golden key
that would unlock the chains around our hearts and bring us unity.
It is no longer my desire to control you or upon you make demands.
It is only a strong desire just to touch your little hands.
I would like to take your little hands and press them to my chest.
I would like to kiss your tender lips and caress your soft, warm breast.
I pray that God grants me my desires before I lose the ability
to ever love again.

The World Would Understand

If the birds in the trees could sing with a voice as sweet as yours,
then the world would understand.
If the sun in the sky could shine as sweetly as your smile,
then the world would understand.
If the stars in the evening sky could dance and twinkle
with the brilliance of the sparkle in your eyes,
then the world would understand.
If all the world could be spectators in my dreams of you,
then the world would understand.
If the world could see the longing in my soul just to hold you close,
then the world would understand.
If you would just open up your heart to me,
then the world would feel my joy.

My Special Friend

I sit and write this letter to my special friend, as
I have no other to whom I can confide,
And with such a friend as you, my feelings I feel I do not have to hide.
You see, I know this woman, her name I won't
reveal, who means so much to me.
You see, I know I love this woman with all that I have inside,
but I keep saying and doing foolish things so I can make her see
just how much I love her and what she truly means to me.
So I write this letter to my special friend to seek some sound advice,
for I hope there is more to love and life than just the tossing of the dice.
How do I describe her? Well, she's beauty beyond compare.
I love to watch the sunlight the way it dances like a halo off her hair.
She's strong, independent, and filled with
confidence, intelligence, and pride,
and she has an inner glow that to the world she cannot hide.
That is why I have this prayer that I will always be closely by her side.
So, my special friend, that is why I turn to you,
so that I may gain some insight or maybe just a clue
so I can stop saying and doing all the foolish things I do.
So you see, my special friend, that is why I come to you,
for no one knows this woman's heart and feelings quite like you.
Yes, I love this woman. Her smile and her
laughter fill my heart like summer air.
I love to watch the moonlight the way it dances like a halo off her hair.
So if you see my angel, then perhaps you just might say
that you received a letter from a humble, love-filled friend today.
You might mention he is working through his insecurities and fears
in hopes of being able just to stand beside her and hold her tender hand
throughout the coming years.
You see in all my life I have never known anyone quite like her.
She is elegance and grace and beauty beyond compare.
No one else has ever touched me or the places
in my heart so deeply as she has.
That is why I come to you to ask for guidance and understanding
to help me in my quest to always be her special friend.

To some it may seem foolish to write this letter like I am.
I only hope that she will know that I will always
love her, the way no other can.
You might ask her to have patience with this simple and humble man,
for every day he's striving to do the best he can.
So you see, my special friend, if you happen to see my angel,
you might mention that everything I do, or try to do,
comes from a heart that is devoted and filled with the truest love,
for no one else has ever meant so much to me like my gentle dove.
So, my special friend, this is why I turn to you,
for I know she's never trusted anyone the way that she trusts you.

Silent Stare

The silence is like thunder as we sit just feet apart.
Neither one is speaking, both afraid to expose their hearts.
They say silence is golden, but this I don't believe,
for if this silence is not broken, our hearts shall surely leave.
So in this deadly silence, I say my secret prayer
and hope that someone answers, that someone
listens, that someone cares.
As we lay side by side, into each others eyes we see,
both trying to see the future and if we're meant to be.
At times we gaze with confidence, at other times with doubts and fears.
All I could ever ask is to spend with you my life and years.
When I gaze into your eyes, I know the answers are not there.
I think you feel the same as me, looking through a silent stare.

The Choice

There's a star in the east.
There's a star in the west.
Both cause emotions of love and unrest.
Now I sit at times and wonder what it is I need to do.
Then at once the answer came so quickly.
I had finally passed the test.
It's now time to release you,
for my heart belongs to the star that shines and sparkles
in the skies above the west.

Three Wishes

They say that God grants wishes and helps our prayers come true.
I would ask God grant three wishes concerning my love for you.
My first wish would be, whether near or far apart,
to always carry your love like a jewel
that's always treasured and protected within the beating of my heart.
My second wish would be that, through the sunshine
or the storms, our love will never fail,
but that with each new challenge, our love will
just grow stronger, forever to prevail.
On this day of St. Valentine's, my third wish would be
that you would pledge your life and love to only me.
So that on that single promise, I would pledge the same to you,
that throughout this life and all eternity, I
will always love and stand by you.

Alone in Love

At times I feel so all alone, even in a crowd.
It's as if no one hears me, even though I'm crying painfully and loud.
I ask my God for answers to questions that I ask,
then wonder if he hears me and if he'll answer back.
At times I feel I'm floating on a sea of emptiness, confusion, and dismay,
even though the one I love is so close, but yet so far away.
So I call upon the angels to help this woman understand
that if she'd give me half a chance, by her I'd proudly stand.

Your Picture

As the days and weeks pass by me, I find my sorrows been replaced.
If it wasn't for you picture, I could scarce recall your face.

As I look upon this empty shell that used to be your home,
I can barely feel your presence since you left me here alone.

As I look upon the objects that used to be our life,
I find they have no meaning since you no longer are my wife.

The thoughts of you that once held me so closely to your side,
no longer seem important since you no longer are my bride.

I feel the memories passing, this truth I cannot erase.
If it wasn't for your picture, I could scarce recall your face.

I know these words are empty, I know that they're not true,
for no one else could hold my heart, no one else but you.

As the days and weeks go by us, it's your love I still embrace,
just waiting for the moment when once again and throughout time
I shall gaze upon the beauty of your grace.

Imprisoned

I feel our time together is coming to an end.
The only thing I asked of you was the one thing
that completely, you could not give.
You would bring it oh, so close to me, and then you would pull it back.
The words to gain it fully, I always seemed to lack.
God knows how much I love you, and the angels know how much I care,
but the burden of this heartache seems unjust and hard to bear.
I pray that I'm mistaken, that we haven't been in vain,
for in this saddened heart of mine, I am imprisoned and in pain.

Lost Moments

There are moments and events that pass at times so slowly,
yet at other times so fast.
When at last the time should arrive
and love comes into your life like a beautiful song and dance,
cradle it, protect it, defend it with your life.

For like the moments and events that pass at times so slowly,
yet at other times so fast,
a love that is not cherished, is a love that cannot last.
For in a hurried moment, in an instant, in a flash,
the times that once were cherished are now buried in the past.

Trust

Do you hear but fail to listen?
Do you look but fail to see?
The love that comes from spirit,
the love that comes from deep within me.
Do you look for love but fail to find it
like so many lonely faces that we see?
Are you looking for that silent gaze from someone in the crowd
that says they understand your fear and vulnerability?
You fear to open up your heart and find a love that's real.
Are you looking for that silent gaze that says it's safe to feel?

Changes of Your Heart

You are the sun that brightens my days.
You are the moon that illuminates my nights.
You are my first conscious thought as I awaken.
You are my last conscious thought as I drift off to sleep.
You are my love, my friend, and my confidant.
You are the radiance that glows from my heart.
But now the tides have shifted, no longer shall we be.
The heart that beat with such joy is now a dead, decaying thing.
So as I turn to walk away, one last glimpse of you I take,
knowing that I will love you through all time,
within the tortured chambers of an empty, broken mind.

Reunion

I know the day is drawing near when two lonely hearts will reunite.
As we rejoin in love's sweet bliss, two hearts will beat again with joy.
When once again we will walk hand in hand,
down the road of life together.
As the world awaits this wondrous day, this day of our reunion,
the day we reunite.

Nameless

She walked into my life for a moment, that was all,
but in that golden moment she captured all of me.

Like an apparition so silently she appeared,
and only for a moment, happiness and laughter reappeared.

For the moment she was nameless, for I know not from where she came,
but when she left, my heart she had quickly claimed.

Her hair was brown, and her eyes were green.
Her face a childlike round,
with lips that looked as tender and soft as fresh spun silk.

Only for a moment did she enter into my life,
but I will hold that gentle vision until I find her,
and together we can travel through this life

You and I

We've shared a lot of lifetimes together, you and I.
I believe that's why we see so many things the
same, yet different, but mostly eye to eye.
Our lifetimes seem to run the same, then split apart for lengths of time,
but we always meet again in another space and time.
At times I am the leader, and other times it is you,
but in this life, as in others, we are always searching for the truth.
There's times we have direction, and there's times that we feel lost,
but we always charge boldly forward, no matter what the cost.
We've spent a lot of energy, building dreams then moving on.
It seems there's nothing that can hold us; we're here and then we're gone.
It's not for you and I that I fear, it's for those who cross our path.
Because you damn well know at times they will feel our verbal wrath.
I believe that is the reason why we keep coming back.
Until we learn some patience and compassion for the meek,
you and I will keep coming back here until we learn to share
our strength with those whom we consider weak.
So let's hope we learn our lessons, let's hope we get it right,
because I'm really getting tired and would
like to journey to the eternal light.
We've walked this world together in other lifetimes,
you and I.

Crossing Over

Death

Why do we fear dying?
Why do we fear death?

The only thing they bury is the shell we leave behind,
for they can never bury the power of the mind.

So release your fear of dying and release your fear of death,
for it's only one more journey, the soul in search of its new quest.

Don't Cry

Don't cry for me, my children, as they lay this shell to rest,
for the body that lies before you is just the temple that I used.

Don't cry for me, my children. Please try to understand.
Death is just another journey for all of mortal man.

Don't cry for me, my children, for I shall never travel far.
I shall always be here with you to dry your falling tears,
for I will always be here with you to guide you through you fears.

So don't cry for me, my children,
for I shall always be here through the passage of the years.

Last Ride

As I saddle up my memories to go on my last ride,
I know the time is drawing near to cross the other side.

So as I open up the book to the pages of my life,
I look back on all the sorrow and the pain I caused in life.

If I have one wish coming, it would be to have
the time to set things straight,
to tell them all I'm sorry for the anger and the hate.

I would pray that they forgive the weakness of the man
and ask them please to try to understand.

As I saddle up my memories to go on my last ride,
I can feel my vision fading, the heavy breathings hard to hide.

I pray they can forgive the empty arrogance and pride.
They were only used to cover up the fears and doubts I held inside.

How I hunger for my children and my pretty little wife
to be here by my side as I journey from this painful, lonely life.

Now as my heart beat grows fainter and my eyes no longer see,
I pray my wife and children can only see the man I tried to be.

So as I lay here dying and I take in my last breath,
I wish to tell the ones I love to have no fear of death.

For it's only one more journey. It's only one more ride.
So I say goodbye to those I love as I cross the other side.

Angels and Spirit Guides

Whispers

There's an angel on my shoulder who keeps whispering in my ear.
She tells me not to worry, to release my anger and my fears.
She tells me not to bottle up my stresses from the day
but to bless each and every one of them,
then just send them on their way.
She's always speaking to me, even when I refuse to hear.
She's an ever-gentle presence; I know she's always near.
My angel works so calmly to give me guidance in my life.
It's taken her some years to make me understand
that only through the love of self can I become a gentle, loving man.
So as I take this pen in hand and write these words to you,
I send this simple message that God sends his gift to you,
his gift of faith and guidance, his gift of love for all of you.

Lonely Post

At times I feel like a soldier, standing guard upon the gate,
trying hard to stop the emotions of love, anger, fear, and hate.
Through years of deep suppression, of holding back the flood,
like a soldier at a lonely post, I once again have to face my fears alone.
So I call upon the enlightened ones, the ones who have gone before,
to guide me through places in my heart and
mind where I have never gone before.

The Chamber

I was guided to a chamber through darkened
corridors. By what, I could not see.
I only felt their presence. One before, one behind.
We traveled through the mazes, the hallways of my mind
until we came upon a chamber where I was given peace of mind.
I sat before a council. As they listened, I explained
about my fears and inner doubts.
They gathered all about me and wiped away my tears,
and when next I awoke, I became aware that
they had also relieved me of my fears.

Angels

Angels are among us, but through our eyes, the angels we may fail to see.
It's only through awareness that their presence may be felt.

Yes, angels are among us, to help us through our sorrow and despair.
They are also there in times of happiness and joy.
When we ask our God for guidance and protection from above,
He sends his silent angels on the wings of snow white doves.

Angels are among us, of this I have no doubt,
for many times I've felt their presence
and heard their silent messages from within.

My Thoughts of You

You have always been a constant force upon my journey through this life.
You have always been there for me through my happiness and strife.

You have patiently given me guidance through
my anger, depression, and self-hate,
In my heart, I know they have engraved your name in gold
on eternity's shimmering gate.

I thank you for your selfless love you have always shown to me.
I wish I had the strength in words to tell you what that has meant to me.

If I could have just one wish and have it become true,
my wish would be that everyone in the world
could have a spirit guide as wonderful as you.

You have always had a special place inside my heart.
So I thought I would let you know that these
are just my special thoughts,
my special thoughts of you.

Words to Inspire

Lifetime

We only have one lifetime in the current body we possess,
so while you're in there, try to use it to your best.

Love of Life

Life is to be lived and loved.
It's a time of growing and changing and
allowing all that is good to come.
Live your life to its fullest.
Enjoy all it has to give.

Secrets

The answers to the secrets of the universe are not that hard to find.

Just unlock the hidden doors, and dare to look
into the contents of your mind.

Time

The limits of time are only on the face of a clock.

We are limited by time only because of our teachings.

For eternity has no limits because eternity is never ending.

Perfection

The idea of perfection is only a concept in our minds.
What may seem perfect to you may not seem that way to me.
So remember the opinions of others are just that—their opinions.
So what I'm saying is, don't base your self-worth on their opinions
or the things that they may say,
for they're only their opinions, and like the sands,
in time they blow away.
In your heart you are the only one who knows what is right and perfect
just for you.

Release

Have you ever felt the urge to just jump up and dance about?

Did you ever feel that in those times, you had
released some fears and self-doubt?

Believe

If you can think it, you can do it. The power lies inside of you.

If you can dream it, you can create it. There is nothing you can't do.

Believe in who you are and what you came to do.

Limits

The only limits in this life are the limits we have placed upon ourselves.

So dare to dream, then dare to do!

For there are no limits on the soul that lives inside of you.

I Am

I am a poet, a writer, a minister of truth.
I am a guide, a teacher, a source of inner light.
I am radiance, abundance, a joy beyond compare.
I am here! I am now!
And I shine from within each and every one of you.

Cosmic Winds

The cosmic winds are blowing through the consciousness of man.
Now it's time to heed the message; it's time we try to understand.
This planet we call Mother Earth has been neglected and abused.
The ancient ones are stirring up these mighty winds.
They're sending down enlightenment in hopes that we will comprehend.
If we don't make some changes, we will bring about our own end.
The cosmic winds are blowing all across the land.
They're blowing through the hearts and the consciousness of man.
The cosmic winds are telling us that the healing of our Mother Earth
starts with you and me.

The Man Behind the Wood

You've lived a life of trial, heartache, and despair,
always feeling that the cards life dealt were unjust, bitter, and unfair.
You've tried to find your happiness through the teachings of God's word,
but through the interpretations of mere man,
his words were grossly misunderstood.
You tried to find some meaning by listening
to the man behind the wood,
and once again I stress to you, God's words were grossly misunderstood.
God's teachings are on pure love, a love that grows within the self,
not on fears of damnation and the impurities we've all felt.
God's words were meant to teach us how to love and how to care,
to look upon our fellow man with a heart filled with a willingness
of how to give and how to share.
Through the lack of understanding of the man behind the wood,
he preaches on your terrors and your fears to increase his worldly good.
For there is no place in God's great realm for
those that distort his holy truth.
All that God is asking is that you look inside
yourself to find his wisdom and his truth.
God's word is meant to teach us how to have
patience, faith, and trust and how to care
for all the souls around us, on this earth that we all share.
So don't listen so intently to the man behind the wood,
but take a hold of God's gentle hand and look
inside yourself to find your higher good.
He's asking you to stop looking to the outer
world for the peace you cannot find,
but that you will take the journey within
yourself to find your peace of mind.

Paths That Crossed

Expression of You

I always watch with wonder and joy within my heart and thoughts
at the expressions that dance upon your face,
from the sparkle in your pure blue eyes
to a smile that's been kissed by an angel as it plays across your face.

The little way you twist your lip that never
fails to put a smile in my heart.
The little chorus in your laughter or just the way that you say "huh!"

My heart beats with such excitement at the mere mention of your name
or when you walk into the room.

You always cause a stirring when you walk into the room,
for no one else has the presence, the very essence that is you.

I have never known anyone who has the ability to touch so many lives,
but the one you have touched the most is
the one who writes these words.

I wait with anticipation of the day I can finally reveal to you
those feelings I have held within the confines of heart.

I stand in waiting for the day that for the first time
I can hold your hand, so that through my touch you will feel what I hold
so tenderly inside my very soul for you.

Unveiling

I held a dream within my soul of an unveiling of our love,
an expression of my desire.

I watched the dream unfold while in blissful slumber did I rest,
while gently placing kisses upon the swelling of your breast.

I dream of a day when love will at last open up the wonders of the world
so that we can feel to express what we both hold
in the secret places of our hearts.

I long for the day I can freely tell you what it is I hold
so tightly with in my chest, of how I long to kiss your tender lips.

In all my life I have never known anyone like you.
So I hold onto the dream within my soul until the unveiling of our love
can freely be expressed.

Thoughts of You

Is it just the silence of the night as I sit here
with my thoughts lost in you,
or is it just the beating of my heart that pounds in rhythm with yours?

I sit in silent contemplation; my mind is just adrift as my thoughts of you
drift upward like prayers on golden wings.

Each time that we're together is a time I truly do embrace,
for each moment we're together allows me the
time to gaze upon your angelic face.

As I sit in quiet contemplation and reflect on this year as it has passed,
I look with wonder and amazement at how we have progressed.

Two people brought together by the choices we both have made,
we worked together side by side when the first feelings began to show.
Now I sit with a picture of you inside my
heart that I am sure will never fade.

I look forward to the moments that we share
when we both open up our hearts
and share our thoughts and interests we both
have had upon this journey we call life.
We seem to both be waiting for the other to say
the words I believe that we both feel.

The two of us, I know, want to say more than
we do. Each of us waiting for the other
to say those tender words, both of us uncertain
what the reaction from the other
just might be.

So I sit in silent contemplation and call upon
the ancient gods to give us guidance
and direction as we begin this journey in our love.

Reality of the Heart

Is what I am feeling real or just a dream?
If this is only a dream, then I pray that I never awaken.
When I think of you, there is such a peace and joy that floods
through my very soul.

Is what I am feeling just a fantasy of the heart?
If this is, then I pray that the fantasy never ends.
For just the mention of your name or just a glimpse of you
causes a celebration within my heart.

I know that we're just beginning. I know that we're brand new.
But if the time we've spent together should grow into something more,
then I make this simple pledge, that I will give my
heart and love to no one else but you.

I spend my nights alone, with my thoughts adrift with a vision of you.
The moments that we are together, I feel that
each time you look into my eyes,
you can see what I am trying to conceal.

The reality of my heart is that I am falling
so very deeply in love with you.
I've never said the words to you because you are not free.
My very special angel, how I long to say those three little words
to the one who holds my dreams.

I ask the angels and my guides to let my dreams come true,
to allow me to express and share all the love
I hold that is waiting just for you.
My very special angel, how I long to hold you
in my arms, how I long to feel
your gentle breath upon my face. I pray that one day soon,
your tender kisses I shall taste.

I call upon the ancient gods of love to look down upon this man

and say he has finally learned the lessons they sent him here to learn,
that love is to be shared and expressed between a woman and a man.

I call upon the ancient gods to hear the meditations of this simple man,
to send down the power to fulfill the desire of his heart
and allow his heart to beat with love and joy
from daylight and through the dark.

Never in My Life

Never in my life did I expect a dream like you,
the beauty of your smile, the chorus in your voice,
the sparkle in your eyes that seems to look in to my very soul.

Never in my life did I expect a dream like you.
The feelings I have for you are so passionate and real.
I do not know when or how the time will come
that they'll be allowed to be expressed,
but until that moment comes I will hold them
within the heartbeats of my chest.

Never in my life did I believe I would ever feel this way again,
but since we've met desire and passion stir anew,
for never in my life did I expect a dream like you.

Two Hearts

I long for the companionship two hearts can share,
the exchange of a loving smile or the moment of a heartfelt gaze.

I long for the tender loving touch two hearts can share
throughout the day, for the gentle loving caress
that says together we both are safe.

I long to share the sunsets and, yes, even the cloudy days,
for when our time comes for us to be together,
our lives will always be this way.

I long to hold your gentle hand and kiss your fingertips,
and as I look across this table, how I long to kiss your tender lips.

I long to hold you in my arms as I do each night within my dreams.

If I Could

If I could paint a picture of you,
it would be of the sun rising in the morning and setting in the evening,
only to give way to the moon as it rises above the mountaintops.

If I could paint a picture of you,
it would be of the stars dancing in the twilight skies,
or it would be the way a breath of wind moves
the leaves upon the trees in perfect time.

If I could paint a picture of you,
it would be of the way a smile plays upon your
lips or of the sparkle in your eyes.
It would be of the way you move with elegance and grace.

If I could paint a picture of you,
it would be so I could always look upon the loveliness of your face.

If I could paint a picture of you and I,
it would be of two hearts celebrating in the rapture of our love.

You Already Have Me

Like a fantasy of the heart,
I have held you in my arms and tasted your sweet and gentle love.
Like a fantasy of the heart,
I have held you and listened to the little murmurs that you make,
like the soft and silent cooing of the morning dove.

You always tell me that you want me,
as I fulfill the needs within your soul.
So please listen, when I'm with you, to the words of love
that tumble from my lips.

You always say you want me,
so please listen when I say
that you have always had me since our time began.

So please listen when I say the words that tumble from my heart,
that you have always had me
from the very start.

Wherever life may take us,
whether together of apart, please remember, my sweet angel,
that you have always had me,
from the very start.

Awaiting the Call
(A Prince in a Fairy Tale)

I love a special lady, her name the angels know.
She feels like she is frozen; she's looking for the way
to the path she needs to take to find her way to happiness
that is waiting just a tender heartbeat away.

Like the prince from a fairy tale, I'm looking for the way
and time to place the kiss of love and passion
that will welt the ice away.

Like the prince I am sitting on my stallion,
the horse that will carry us on our way,
to a life of love and happiness
as our angels guide our way.

The time is getting closer for this prince of love and light
to emerge and lift this lady,
the princess of his life.

The stallion is standing, his muscles tense and taut,
waiting for the word from God to send him charging forward
to claim his princess, who awaits.

The stallion's blood is surging through his veins like a river under flood.
His hooves are dancing in anticipation
for the word to charge that he awaits.

The prince sits upon the saddle with a heart so full of love,
just waiting for the words so he can charge
and claim his gentle dove.

His hand rests upon the hilt of the sword that he will draw
when the call from the angels gives the word to charge.

The stallion's chomping at the bit. His hooves are dancing all about

with energized anticipation, just waiting for the call
that will carry his prince to victory, love, and life.

The prince sits upon the back of his stallion,
gently stroking the stallion's neck,
with a knowing that the princess who has claimed his love
is just a breath away.

So the prince sits upon the stallion, just waiting for the word
that will carry him to love and happiness
when he claims his princess to be his partner throughout life.

Believe in yourself and all that you can do...

Remember!

www.ingramcontent.com/pod-product-compliance
Lightning Source LLC
Chambersburg PA
CBHW020010050426
42450CB00005B/399